Rip-off to Refund

By Josh Fulkerson

Disclaimer

This book is designed to provide information on obtaining a refund after being ripped off. This information is provided and sold with the knowledge that the publisher and author do not offer any legal or other professional advice. In the case of a need for any such expertise consult with the appropriate professional. This book does not contain all information available on the subject. This book has not been created to be specific to any individual's or organizations' situation or needs. Every effort has been made to make this book as accurate as possible. However, there may be typographical and or content errors. Therefore, this book should serve only as a general guide and not as the ultimate source of subject information. This book contains information that might be dated and is intended only to educate. Names, characters, businesses, places, events and incidents are either the products of the author's imagination or used in a fictitious manner. Any resemblance to actual persons, living or dead, or actual events is purely coincidental. The author and publisher shall have no liability or responsibility to any person or entity regarding any loss or damage incurred, or alleged to have incurred, directly or indirectly, by the information contained in this book. You hereby agree to be bound by this disclaimer or you may return this book within the guarantee time period for a full refund.

Table of Contents

Foreword

Someone I know, with whom I am very close, signed up for a gym membership with a one year contract. We will call her Jane. The sales representative seemed to be very friendly and very animated and sold Jane all the benefits of the gym membership such as being open 24 hours, unlimited usage of the gym, all the different types of exercise equipment, an indoor pool, and free childcare just to name a few. Jane was sold and she signed up for a one year contract.

Jane attended the gym three to five times per week to perform her exercise routines and dropped off her daughter in the childcare room prior to beginning her workout. Everything seemed to be going well and Jane was happy to be in better shape.

After two months of regularly attending the gym she showed up one day, dropped off her daughter in the childcare, and was approached by a gym employee. The employee told her that she had not been paying for the childcare usage and that she was not permitted to drop off her daughter in the childcare room until she signed up for the childcare program, which would cost an additional $10 per month.

Wait a minute! The sales representative told her that childcare was included in the gym membership. Jane tried to explain this to the employee, but the employee did not believe her. Jane marched over to the sales representative's office and he denied ever informing her that childcare was free.

Jane chose not to pay the ten dollars and not complete her workout for the day. She called the gym back the same day and spoke with the manager of the gym and she explained the situation to her in hopes that she would rectify this problem. The manager gave her the same response as the employee and did not believe her that the sales representative lied to her. Jane demanded that she be allowed to utilize childcare for free for the remaining ten months of her contract since she was told it was included. She tried to explain to the manager that this was a bait and switch tactic, but the manager did not care and would not provide her with free childcare.

A lot of people would have given up at this point and either agree to pay $10 per month or hire a babysitter. Jane was smart, she did not stop here. She called the corporate office of the gym and she explained the situation to them. Although they were more sympathetic to her situation they still did not agree to provide her with free childcare.

Jane still did not stop there. She knew this gym wanted to keep a good reputation, especially with so much competition around. She decided to execute the steps in this book. The gym representatives were tough, but after Jane completed the fourth step, they finally relented and allowed her to utilize childcare for free for the remainder of the contract period.

This is a true story and stories similar to this happen all the time. Unfortunately, more often than not, the customer loses out because they give up too quickly or they fail to execute the proper steps to obtain satisfaction. That is where this book helps. The steps in this book allow you to reach the highest levels of the company where you have a much better chance of a refund and they allow you to leverage the company's desire for a good reputation, in order to obtain a refund.

Introduction

At one time or another in life, all of us have been ripped off in a business transaction or two. Perhaps we paid too much for a product or service, perhaps the product or service was subpar or shoddy, or maybe we were bait and switched. There are as so many ways we can be ripped off, but in most cases we can and should get a refund.

Just as there are many ways we can be ripped off, there are also many ways we can turn our rip-off into a refund or exchange. Throughout the remainder of this book, we will refer to refunds, exchanges of product, repairs, desired actions, service do-overs, etc. simply as a "refund." In other words, the word "refund" will be a general term used to describe any and all forms of customer satisfaction after a rip-off.

Why am I writing this e-book? Well, it's quite simple. You see, everybody gets ripped off at least a few times during their life, but in far too many cases they don't get a refund. I really doubt it's because they don't feel like bothering with it. I believe if you asked anyone who was recently ripped off if they would like their money back, most would say "yes." Unfortunately most people don't get a refund because they don't know how to take the proper steps and that is why I wrote this book.

Over the past several years, I have been ripped off or highly dissatisfied in a number of business transactions. Through trial and error I discovered what works and what doesn't work as far as getting a refund. I would consider myself having mastered the skills of flipping a rip-off into a refund and I want to teach those same skills to you. I have read and heard so many rip-off stories through friends, family, and even on the internet and sadly most of those stories did not end happily for the customer. I always get flustered and ask them "what steps did you take to try to get your money back?" and I usually hear an answer that goes something like the following:

- *-"I called customer service and they refused to help me, I asked for a supervisor and the supervisor still said no, I guess I won't buy from them anymore and now I am out $200.00"*

- *"I went back to the store and spoke to the manager, and he said he couldn't exchange my TV because it's been over 30 days since I bought it, but it stopped working twice for the same reason and the warranty is almost up. I guess I will have to buy a new one if it breaks again."*

- *"I went to the hotel that I reserved online through (a third party airline/hotel booking sight) and the hotel said they had no record of my reservation. I already paid (third party hotel sight) in advance and they won't give me a refund. I guess I will have to pay for another room now."*

- *"The gym lied to me and they told me that onsite childcare is free with my membership, now they are telling me I have to pay extra for childcare and I am locked in my contract for another 9 months, I can't afford to pay extra, I don't know what I will do, I guess I am stuck."*

- *"I signed up for a monthly DVD subscription and I was enrolled in their music and book club without my consent for which they are charging me additional monthly fees to my credit card. I called the merchant and they told me that in the small print of my contract it explained I would be automatically enrolled in their music and book club unless I opted out up front. The supervisor on the phone told me they have a "no refund" policy. I guess I should have read the small print, now I am out $50"*

Now when I hear those stories, I immediately think of ways that these customers could have easily obtained a refund. That is exactly why I am writing this book. In fact, I feel obligated to write this book because it frustrates me like nothing else every time I hear a rip-off story that goes unresolved. Instead, I would love to hear more and more rip-off stories where the customer takes control and is successfully refunded in the end.

The skills I teach in this book can resolve almost any type of rip-off. However, these skills will NOT work for the following scenarios:

-employment issues
-IRS issues
-State or Local Tax Board Issues
-lawsuits
-wage garnishments or levies
-problems with any government entities

There are different methods for resolving the above issues and unfortunately I am not experienced in any of them so please look elsewhere for help in those areas. You can try my methods on the above, but don't be surprised if they don't work.

What this book is not:

This book is not intended for you to take advantage of companies by implying that a rip-off took place when it didn't. Quite simply, if you have buyer's remorse on an item you purchased and you are past the return policy, do not try to return the product to the store and do NOT follow the steps in this book to try to get them to change their mind. If the product stopped working more than once and you are concerned it will break again after the warranty expires, then that's another story and by all means fight for your refund.

This book is not legal advice. There are attorneys who can help you with that, and I may be bright, but I am not bright enough to be an attorney. ☺

This book is not intended to encourage dishonesty toward a company. Don't ever use these methods to lie or stretch the truth about your rip-off in order to maximize your refund by taking advantage of the company. Stick to the facts, they always work better in the long run.

This book is not a "get even" book or an anti-business or anti-corporation book. There are many great companies that have great mission statements and thrive on providing excellent value and excellent customer service. Companies provide us with necessary products and services that we need in our everyday lives. They provide us with jobs and they keep our economy vibrant and strong.

This book is only intended to resolve rip-offs and to resolve them quickly.

For best results, I recommend following the four steps outlined in this book in order from step one to step four. Do not skip to a later step because refunds are often granted within the first two steps.

In every step of this book, a sample letter or sample conversation based on that step will be posted at the end of that step. The scenario will be a banking customer who was charged 4 overdraft fees of $35 each ($140) because he was locked out of his online banking due to unauthorized logins and didn't have access to see his bank account online for three days. Even though he tried to keep track of his expenses offline, he missed an automatic transaction. We will call our customer John, he is very financially responsible. He has a good credit score and has never been charged overdraft fees in the 3 plus years he has been banking with XYZ Bank. The bank recognizes that he's been banking with them for 3 years, but they will not reverse his overdraft fees because his average daily balance is $1500, and they require a $2000 average daily balance (they will not divulge this to John since banks frown upon customers knowing their fee reversal matrix). John didn't have access to his account online and he feels that his bank should cut him a break because he would have seen that automatic transaction if he had online access. Being charged $140 in overdraft fees will cause a serious financial burden for John if he can't get those fees waived.

Please read each sample letter at the end of each step and try to implement these letters or conversations into your own rip-off scenario.

With that being said, I am happy to jump into the meat of the book with both feet. Enjoy!

Step 1

Contacting the Company

Contacting the company should always be the first step to take when you've been ripped off or wronged in anyway. Why?

First, you want to give the company a chance to right the wrong they have committed. Simply going after their reputation from the get-go without giving them a chance to fix it is ineffective and will only make you look bad. Also, there is a chance that you will be refunded on your first phone call and that will save you a lot of time and effort. Who doesn't want to save time and effort?

Now, when it comes to contacting the company, there is a right way and a wrong way to do it.

The wrong way to do it is to call customer service and yell and curse at the first person who answers the phone. Having worked several years in customer service myself, being belligerent with the company's rep will get you nothing but a dial tone or eternal hold music. It is true that sometimes the Customer Service Rep or supervisor may get you what you want just to get you off the phone, but that is the exception, not the rule.

When you call the company, the best thing you can do is to remain calm and cool. Be polite to the first rep who answers the phone. I understand that it's not easy, especially if you had a horrible experience or lost a lot of money. However, being polite will get you far in most cases. Customer service reps deal with irate people all day long, so if you call up and you are that one polite customer, you will stand out. They will do everything they can to resolve your problem to your desire. If they can't, they will often volunteer to let you speak to their Supervisor. If they don't, politely request that you speak to their supervisor.

Whether you are speaking with the customer service rep or the supervisor you must do the following:

1. Give them your first and last name. If needed, let them authenticate you for security purposes (i.e. account number, last four of social, phone number etc.) and be 100 percent cooperative during this process. The quicker you can get through this, the quicker you can reach your desired resolution. I can't tell you how many times I have had irate customers call me and they are so upset that they refuse to cooperate during the authentication process. They get frustrated because I can't help them until I know it's "really them," the call ends, and no resolution is reached. Don't be that person, instead help them help you and everybody wins.

2. Politely, clearly, and simply state your problem and why you believe you were ripped off. Don't complicate this step by over explaining. Leave your feelings out of it other than stating to the rep that you are frustrated. Don't insult the company and especially don't insult the customer service rep, the more respect you show to them, the more willing they will be to make sure your problem is resolved.

3. Politely, clearly and simply state your desired resolution whether it's a refund, exchange, a free service call, repair, etc. Be reasonable in your desired resolution, but at the same time, don't be ashamed to ask for exactly what you want. Do not make threats to the company or to the representative, for example don't threaten to sue the company or to get a lawyer, because many companies have a policy that if a customer threatens legal action, the representative will no longer be able speak to or assist the customer. This will dramatically lengthen the time to reach your resolution. Remember, you want your refund as quickly as possible.

4. If your desired resolution is reached, great, you have nothing more to do, thank the rep and move on.

5. If your desired resolution is not reached even after speaking to a supervisor, politely ask to speak to a higher up supervisor. Keep going until

you are told that you can't speak to anyone higher. Do not end the call in an angry outburst of obscenities, stay calm and cool and end the call. Get the name of the rep or supervisor with whom you spoke and write it down. You will need it later.

Your first contact with the company may not be over the phone. It may be a visit to the store. If the product that you bought is within warranty, there shouldn't be any problem getting a repair or replacement, but if you purchased an extended warranty and they refuse to honor it (for example) or if the product doesn't live up to the promises the advertisement or sales representative made, then you will likely have more of a challenge. So, you would use a similar tactic as on the phone. First you would speak to an employee of the store, if it was a large ticket item, you would speak with your sales representative. Remember to be polite and to not make a scene. If the employee cannot provide you with an exchange or refund, ask for the manager. Explain your problem nicely to the manager, if the manager will not provide you with an exchange or refund, ask to speak with the highest manager in the store. If you have exhausted all levels of management in the store without success, then you need to go on to the next step.

Your first contact may not be over the phone or at the store. Perhaps you made your purchase through an online company with no store and no customer service phone number, only an email address. Email them your issue and remember to be polite in your email. Give them no more than 2 days longer than their promised turn-around time. If they do not respond go to the next step. If they do respond, but they decline refunding you or exchanging the product then go to the next step.

Resolution is not usually reached on the first call, visit to the store, or email and that's okay because there are more steps to take that are outlined throughout this book that will likely help you get your desired refund. Like I said earlier, I recommend going in the order the steps are laid out because there is a good chance that you will be granted your refund within the first two steps. The later steps are more involved and take more time.

Below is a sample conversation from our sample customer John who was introduced at the end of the Introduction of this book. He is calling XYZ Banking Customer Service to see if they will reverse his overdraft fees that he incurred because he did not have online access to his bank account. You will notice that John is polite, non-insulting, and non-threatening as he should be in this step.

John: Hi, my name is John and I am calling because I was charged four overdraft fees on my account due to not having online access to my accounts and not seeing an automatic transaction, I kept track of all my other transactions, so I wanted to see if I can get those fees reversed.

XYZ Rep: I'll be happy to look into those, I need to ask you a few questions to verify your identity?

John: Yes, go ahead.

(authentication process)

XYZ Rep: Okay, I understand you want to see if we can reverse your overdraft fees?

John: Yes, I've been an XYZ customer for over 3 years and I've never been charged overdraft fees before, and I wanted to see if you can cut me a break, $140 will really hurt me financially.

XYZ Rep: Okay, I looked into your account and unfortunately I am unable to reverse your overdraft fees today. I am very sorry.

John: Okay, please understand that I've been banking with you for over 3 years and I could have prevented my account from overdrawing if I was not locked out of my online access to my bank account. Can I please speak to your Supervisor?

XYZ Rep: Yes, one moment

XYZ Supervisor: Hi, I understand you would like to have your overdraft fees reversed?

John: Yes, I've been banking with you for over three years and I have never overdrawn my account before. My online access to my bank account was down and I didn't see an automatic transaction, I kept track of my other transactions, so I would like you to cut me a break.

XYZ Supervisor: My rep is correct, unfortunately we cannot reverse your overdraft fees at this time. Is there anything else I can do for you today?

John: No, there is nothing else. It's too bad that you have chosen not to help me with these fees. Thanks for your time. Bye.

Step 2

The Social Media Attack

Let's face it, Social Media has changed the lives of countless people throughout the world both positively and negatively. We now have a way to connect to everyone we know at the click of a mouse. We have also experienced a big loss of privacy and everything we say and do is public. Social Media includes sites like Facebook, Twitter, Google Plus, Youtube, and many others.

In this book we will focus on Facebook since it is by far the most popular form of Social Media.

Lots of companies, especially big ones use Facebook to promote themselves. They create fan pages where people can "like" them and post comments and questions. This creates a lot of exposure for the company, which can be very helpful for them to get their message out without spending millions of dollars on advertising.

This also creates a convenient way for you as a rip-off victim to quickly get the attention of someone high up in the company to resolve your issue. Because companies have so much exposure on Facebook, if someone writes a complaint about a poor experience or a poor product, it is in their best interest to take care of the problem as quickly as possible. Most companies place someone fairly high up in the company to monitor their Facebook fan page and to monitor activity that may negatively affect their reputation. So if you post a complaint on their fan page, you will often get a response within minutes, sometimes within seconds. They will usually comment on your post with an apology and with a promise to speak with you to work something out. After that they will usually send you a private message providing their direct contact number. When you call them and nicely explain to them your situation, they will often provide you with the exact refund you requested, because the last thing they want you to do is to go back on their Facebook fan page and post another negative comment. After they take care of you, they will often ask you to write something positive about your experience calling them. Keep in mind that when you post your complaint on the company's Facebook fan page, it will appear on your timeline and your friends will be able to see it. I actually have found this to be helpful, because my friends have posted comments in my support on the complaint and it only puts more pressure on the company to refund me in full.

So here is what you should do. Go to facebook.com and go to the search bar at the top. Type in the name of the company who ripped you off. Quite a few search results will pop down. Choose the result that has the highest number of fans, usually this is the company's main fan page. Most fan pages will have a place to leave a post, some fan pages will not have a place to post, and some will require that you "like" them before posting.

If they do not have a place to post, move to Step 3, unfortunately some companies do not allow posts on their Facebook page. If they require you to like them first, like them, and write your comment. Once you have received a response from them providing you with their contact info, unlike them.

Your comment should be structured in the following way. First, give a one sentence introduction such as "I had a negative experience with one of your retail stores." It should be this simple. Second, describe how you were ripped off and to whom you previously spoke to try and resolve the issue. Lastly, clearly state your desired outcome in no more than two sentences.

When you leave your comment, remember to:

-stick with the facts

-avoid libel (written slander)

-be respectful and don't make a fool of yourself

-keep your comment as brief as possible

When the company representative responds with their contact information, call them the same day if possible. Remember to be respectful and to avoid insults or yelling, the nicer you are to them the better chance of reaching your desired outcome. At the same time make sure you are firm on your desired outcome. They will either refund you in full, offer a partial refund, or not offer you any refund at all. If they offer less than your desired outcome, make sure you will be satisfied with that before you accept it. Only you can determine what is reasonable when they try to settle. If it's not reasonable, firmly but politely decline their offer. You should demand that they give you your full refund. They may counter offer again, they may go ahead and grant your desired outcome, or they may stick with their original offer. If they stick with their original offer, go ahead and end the call and move on to Step 3. Also, if they do not offer you any refund at all, move on to Step 3. Avoid making threats and especially avoid threatening to execute steps 3 and 4. It is always more effective when you surprise them with the next step. Think about it, if you threaten to contact their CEO or go to the Better Business Bureau, they can plan how they will respond and they will be ready for you, do not give them that chance. However, if they are caught by surprise, they will have a limited time to respond and they are more likely to give you a full refund.

If they give you a full refund in this step, you are finished. If they don't, go ahead and move to Step 3.

I want to quickly say something about Youtube. You can make a video on Youtube where you explain and demonstrate your rip-off. It is especially effective if you have a product that failed or broke too quickly

24

because you can video the product and its defect. Be sure to choose effective key words when you post the video. Be sure to also post a link to the video on the company's Facebook fan page to get a quick response.

Below is a sample letter from our sample customer John to XYZ Bank. Customer Service refused to reverse his overdraft fees, so now he's following Step 2 by writing a letter on XYZ's Facebook fan page. Notice that he does not use any slander, libel, or threats.

Hello. I had a negative experience with XYZ Bank that I want to share. I was charged four overdraft fees of $35 each adding up to $140. This is very unusual for me as I am very responsible with my finances. My account was overdrawn because I was locked out of my online access due to unauthorized logins and I didn't see an automatic transaction, but I did keep track of all my other transactions. Being down $140 will really mess up my finances and it will be nearly impossible to pull myself out of the hole. I contacted Customer Service and spoke with a supervisor named Nancy and she informed me they could not reverse any fees. I don't believe that my request is unreasonable. I've been banking with you for over three years, I've never had an overdraft fee, and this really wasn't my fault because I didn't have online access. So, please do the right thing by helping me out today by reversing my four $35 overdraft fees. I will make sure I keep my account from overdrafting again. Thanks

Step 3

Contacting the Ultimate Decision Maker

If you have come this far and you still have not been granted a refund, then it's time to contact the Ultimate Decision Maker, the CEO of the company. Yes, it's time to contact the head honcho. This step may seem intimidating, but trust me, it's much easier than you think. Now these instructions do not work 100% of the time, but they do work most of the time.

You will be sending an email to the CEO that is worded just like your message on the company's Facebook fan page. First, you would give a one sentence introduction such as "I had a negative experience in one of your retail stores." Second, you would describe how you were ripped off. Explain who you spoke to and mention that you spoke with one of the company's representatives on their Facebook fan page. Feel free to copy and paste the Facebook conversation into the body of the email. A few key points to remember when speaking with the CEO:

- this man or woman is the ultimate decision maker, and it does not matter what any other company representative said to you up to this point, because they have the power to override any and all decisions made by anyone else

- because he or she is the ultimate decision maker, you will want to be as kind and as respectful as possible (but do not apologize for your prior actions)

- be very clear and direct on your desired outcome, do not be shy or intimidated

- never insult or be condescending toward the CEO, he or she is not the hourly paid rep you spoke with at customer service, remember that your ultimate goal is to reach your desired outcome, not to start a fight with the head honcho.

Great, now that you know how to write a letter and interact with the CEO, how in the world do you contact the CEO?

You can write a letter to the main corporate office, but you probably do not want to wait a month for a response. So here's a sneaky way to contact the CEO:

Email the CEO

Yes, send an email to the CEO and expect an answer within 24 minutes to 24 hours.

How do you get their email address? It is easier than you think.

Let's say the company's name is AJP Wireless. What you would do is pull up any search engine such as Google or Yahoo. Execute a search on "CEO of AJP Wireless." Several search results should appear on the screen. Search results may include links to corporate profiles, Wikipedia descriptions, or the actual company website, etc.

You should find the CEO's name on more than one of the search results. Check to make sure the information is not outdated, I am sure the ex-CEO will not be of any help. Click through most of the links and you'll be able find out who is the current CEO. Try to get a first name, middle name and last name if at all possible.

Once you have found out the CEO, you will want to find out the company's website address if you do not know it already. Let's say the company's website in this example is ajpwireless.com and let's say the CEO's name is Aaron James Peterson.

What you will do is compose a new email with an appropriate subject line, write out your message to the CEO as described at the beginning of this chapter. In the "to" field of the email, type in every possible variance of email address separated by a semi-colon as follows:

aaron.peterson@ajpwireless.com;
aaron.james.peterson@ajpwireless.com;
aaron.j.peterson@ajpwireless.com;
aaronpeterson@ajpwireless.com;
aaronjamespeterson@ajpwireless.com;
aaronjpeterson@ajpwireless.com etc. etc. etc.

Do not stop there either, if you can think of other ways his email address may be setup, by all means add it. Once you have all email variances in the "to" field, go ahead and click send.

You will get several bounced emails back in your inbox. Open each of the "failed delivery" emails and take note of the failed email address. If there is one email address variance that did not bounce back a "failed delivery" notice, then that email is good and you know it is the CEO's email address.

Congratulations, you successfully emailed the CEO, now you will wait for his or her response. Don't be surprised if the CEO's secretary or another executive responds back to you. Remember to be polite, but firm in explaining your desired outcome. Do not make any threats if he or she does not offer you or denies your desired outcome. They do not need to know what is your next step, it is always best when you can catch them by surprise.

Usually at this point, the CEO will give you what you want. They know you have already spoken to the highest supervisor at customer service, they know you have already posted a Facebook post on the company fan page, and now they know you found a way to contact them. They want this issue to be over. However, if they still say no, then it's time to move to the next step.

Below is a sample email that John will write to the CEO of XYZ Bank. Let's say that the name of the bank's CEO is Russell Jones. You will notice that the email is very similar to the Facebook post in the last step, but with a few added lines.

Dear Russell Jones,

I had a negative experience with XYZ Bank that I want to share with you as the CEO of the bank. I was charged four overdraft fees of $35 each adding up to $140. This is very unusual for me as I am very responsible with my finances. My account was overdrawn because I was locked out of my online banking and I missed an automatic transaction, I did keep track of all my other transactions so I am asking the bank reverse my fees. Being down $140 will really mess up my finances and it will be nearly impossible to pull myself out of the hole. I contacted Customer Service and spoke with a supervisor named Nancy and she informed me they could not reverse any fees. I also posted my story on your Facebook page and I received a response from Julianna at your bank, but she also refused to reverse any overdraft fees. I don't believe that my request is unreasonable. I've been banking with you for over three years, I've never overdrawn my account, and it wasn't my fault because I didn't have online access. Also, $140 is a lot of money to me, and it's not a lot of money to you. So, please do the right thing by helping me out today by reversing my four $35 overdraft fees. I will make sure I *keep my account from overdrawing again. I have enjoyed banking with your bank, but this experience has put a sour taste in my mouth, and I ask that you make this better by helping me. Please respond back by email or call me at (555)555-5555. Thanks*

John

Step 4

The Achilles Heel of Business

What is the Achilles Heel of Business? The Achilles Heel of all businesses is what I like to call the Credit Bureau of all businesses. Just as you want to keep your credit score high and keep any negative items off your credit report, businesses want to keep their score high with this entity known as the Better Business Bureau. We will refer to them as the BBB throughout the remainder of this book.

It will be helpful to know that the BBB has several branches throughout the USA and Canada. Each region has a BBB branch that oversees the businesses in that area. For example, California has six BBB branches serving the various regions of the state. Do you live outside the USA or Canada? In the UK they have "Which?", and no, that is not a typo. In Australia they have the Australian Competition and Consumer Commission (ACCC). It is likely that most modernized countries have some type of consumer agency that can assist with any bad business practices. So if you are reading this book from another country outside the USA or Canada, do a google search on "Better Business Bureau [Country name]" and you should be able to find the equivalent of such in the search results. Since I don't have any experience dealing with these other agencies, we will stick with the BBB in this book.

Let me explain how the BBB operates. They keep a record of company complaints for three years and they assign a grade to the business based off the number of complaints and whether those complaints were resolved or not. Some BBB branches assign letter grades A, B, C, D, and F, while others use Satisfactory or Unsatisfactory. The grading with most branches is pretty harsh. That's good news for you and can be bad news for the business if they run a shady operation. I have seen businesses' grades drop to C or D over only one unresolved complaint.

Now, you may have heard bad rumors about the BBB; that they do not really help, that they are only out there to protect the businesses, that they take bribe money from businesses in exchange for a clean record. Although I do not believe a lot of the negative hype floating around out there, I must mention that not all BBB branches are perfect. Most branches that I have worked with are fair and unbiased, but there are a small number of Branches who side heavily with the business and a small number that side heavily with the consumer. The BBB does not take bribe money, but they do allow businesses to become a BBB Member for a fee. However, they do not allow the businesses to get away with bad business practices just because they are a paid member. In fact, a business can lose their BBB membership if they engage in bad business practices.

Even with all the negative rumors about the Better Business Bureau, you should still utilize their services as most people have had great success with them. Their services are free for you, they earn their money from BBB memberships that businesses pay.

Once you have gone through all the steps and you have reached this point with no success in obtaining your refund, it is time to file a BBB complaint against the business. It should only take you fifteen to twenty minutes to file the complaint. However, it can take up to 30 days for the business to respond to the BBB. It really depends on the company, I have had companies respond as quickly as the next day. On the flipside I have had companies respond on the 29th day. Either way, you are still ripped off at this point and waiting up to 30 days for a possible resolution is better than nothing. So below are the steps to file a BBB complaint against the company (please keep in mind that the BBB may change the look and organization of their website at any time).

1. Go to www.bbb.org

2. Click on "See all BBB Locations" box

3. In the upper right hand corner, type the name of the business in the search box

4. A list of matches will show in the search results. Look for the company name where it says "Headquarters," this is where you will file your

complaint. Click on "file complaint" or you can click the company name if you want to read prior complaints from other rip-off victims. Some big companies such as retail chains and banks will have multiple locations, but always choose the Company Headquarters since you are shooting for top decision makers. If you cannot find the company, it's possible the BBB has no information on them. This is common with new or small businesses that have never had a BBB complaint filed against them. This should be no problem because you can manually add the company information and file your complaint.

5. From here the BBB website will walk you through the complaint process step-by-step. It will ask you questions about the nature of the complaint to make sure it's a valid consumer complaint, it will ask for your contact information, and it will ask you details about your purchase that resulted in a rip-off. It is helpful to have any account numbers or transaction numbers during this phase. It will also ask you about prior attempts to contact the company. This is why it is a good idea to keep track of all representatives with whom you have spoken. If you do not remember their names, don't worry, just write in "Representative" and move on.

6. You will eventually be brought to a point where you will be asked to describe your rip-off. Be sure to keep it brief enough to fit within the allotted number of words, but long enough that it sufficiently describes the problem. Do not state your desired outcome here, there will be another field for that.

7. Once you have typed in your rip-off description, be sure to copy and paste the description into a Word Processor so you can save it. This will not only be useful for future reference, it will also be useful in case your session times out on bbb.org and the description you typed disappears after submitting. Then you will not have to type the rip-off description again, you can just copy and paste it back into the website.

8. Once you have copied and pasted your rip-off description, you will be brought to another box where you will type in your desired outcome. On previous posts I asked you to avoid making threats of next actions you will take if they do not refund you. Here it is different. You've already taken a few steps prior to the BBB Complaint. Be sure to mention this and explain that if your desired outcome is not made that you will continue to take further actions until you receive your desired outcome. It is okay to threaten "possible legal action" or threaten to share your story with the local media.

9. Once you have submitted your complaint, you will be provided with a complaint number. Some BBB offices will allow you to check the status of your complaint using this number through their website.

Once your complaint is submitted, you just wait. The BBB is by far the most effective way to get your rip-off resolved in the way you want. So why do I not suggest you to go directly to the BBB in the beginning? Time. That is my answer, the previous methods can help you get your refund very quickly while the BBB takes up to 30 days. What more? When you complete the prior steps, it only adds more credibility and strength to your BBB complaint. Also the higher-ups in the company have already dealt with you on the previous steps and by now they are tired of assisting you. They will do almost anything to get you off their back, which in most cases will be giving you the refund you desire just so they do not have to deal with you anymore.

When the company finally responds to your complaint, they will usually do it in writing either in the mail, or through the BBB sight. Sometimes they will call you on the phone. After their initial response and offer, you can either accept or reject what they offer you. Sometimes they will give you exactly what you want on the initial response, sometimes they will try to settle for less. If you accept their offer, the BBB case will be closed and you are finished. If you reject their offer, they'll come back with a final response. Often the final response will be your full desired outcome, because they know now that you will accept nothing less.

Just for your information, some companies will act totally surprised that you went to the BBB to file your complaint. Some will try to make you feel guilty or tell you that going to the BBB was "unnecessary" and harmful to their organization. I have six words to say concerning this: "Do not listen to that crap," it's just an act. They want you to feel guilty in hopes that you will accept less than your desired outcome. Do not fall for it. Firmly tell them about all the trouble you went through prior to filing the BBB complaint, emphasize to them that you made the correct decision to go to the BBB, and that you intend to continue further action until you reach your desired outcome.

If you still do not succeed in getting a refund at this point or if the company does not respond to the BBB complaint, then I am very sorry. You are dealing with a very sleazy company and they will take a big hit on their BBB grade just from your unresolved complaint alone. You can try faxing or emailing the CEO the BBB complaint, it is possible the representative who oversees BBB complaints is sleeping on the job.

What if the BBB itself rejects the complaint? I had it happen to me once when I filed a complaint against a company for a billing issue. The BBB will not accept certain complaints and one of those is filing a complaint against a company for charging too much for a product or service. The BBB recognizes that a company has the right to charge whatever price they desire for a product or service. Billing issues or collection issues are different than price issues. They usually have something to do with disagreeing with a bill because you were charged for something you did not receive, a collection department adds on ridiculous amounts of penalties, fees, and interest making it hard to pay off your collection, or a company charges you, but they do not perform the service or provide you the product they promised. If you get rejected for complaining about a price, re-write your complaint to focus on something else other than the price. Emphasize that they made a mistake and charged you for something that you did not order or receive. Emphasize the abusive collection schemes. Emphasize that the company did not perform the service or provide the product for which you paid. Avoid stating that you were "charged" you too much. Some BBB offices will be more lenient on how you word your complaint in a billing dispute while others will shut you down for even mentioning a disagreement on how much they are charging.

After reading this chapter, you may be hesitant about filing a BBB complaint. Do not be hesitant, most of the time it works really well, I just wanted to prepare you for possible bumps in the road with them. To be forewarned is to be forearmed.

Below is a sample letter that John will write to the Better Business Bureau. This letter is in two parts, the first part is the rip-off description and the second part is the desired outcome since the BBB is setup that way. Notice that John uses the word "penalty" rather than "charge" or "fee" because the BBB may drop a complaint if it is in regard to how much a company charges for a service.

Rip-off Description

I am filing a complaint against XYZ bank due to their unwillingness to help me with my overdraft penalties. Due to my being locked out of online banking, I missed an automatic transaction and I was hit with four $35 overdraft penalties ($140) and this will put me in a hole financially where I may never dig myself out. I have been banking with XYZ bank for over three years and I have never overdrawn my account until now. I really don't understand why the bank can't offer me a refund of my overdrafts, especially since it really wasn't my fault. I am financially responsible, I pay all my bills on time, and I've never overdrawn my account before. From my understanding, most banks will provide a one-time waiver of penalties for good customers. I really don't understand why this bank feels they don't need to take care of this.

Desired Outcome

As I requested in my previous complaints. I want a full refund of ALL four overdraft penalties, nothing less.

Anything less than a full refund will result in an unresolved complaint with the Better Business Bureau and further actions will be taken to recover my lost money. The Bank must understand by now that I am not stopping until my penalties are refunded. I have already complained to multiple representatives within the company including the CEO. Please do the right thing and put this complaint behind you by refunding my $140 today.

Conclusion

Once you have completed all four steps, you most likely received your refund. Although it is rare, you may have performed all four steps with no success at all. You do not have to end your quest for a refund at this point, but if you feel it would be a wasted effort to continue, just remember, the business' reputation has taken a nasty hit from these four steps you performed and it is quite possible that their loss is substantially more than the dollar amount you were ripped off.

If you want to continue to pursue a refund, below are some ideas you can try, I did not create chapters for these techniques because I do not have a lot of experience with them, mostly because I had so much success with the four steps.

Here are some ideas you can try:

- You can contact your bank and see if you can open a dispute claim (this will not work if you paid with cash). You may be able to recover some or all of your money depending on whether the bank will have charge-back rights (the right to electronically take their money back from the merchant). I have had to use this process twice in my life, and I was successful both times. Some banks will honor your dispute automatically if it is less than a certain dollar amount (some banks are $35, some are $25, I worked for a bank that honored all disputes under $50). The more you fight for a refund prior to filing your claim, the better chance you have of getting your money back by filing a claim with your bank. Hopefully you documented your actions in the four steps.

- If you can demonstrate or show your defective product or shoddy service in a video, make a video and post the video on Youtube. If you have a blog, post that video on your blog. You may be able to get thousands of hits on your video within weeks. You can write another email to the CEO and post a link to the Youtube video and offer to take down the video in exchange for your desired refund.

- You can post your complaint on consumer complaint websites such as complaints.com, complaintsboard.com, rippedoffonline.com, or ripoffreport.com.

- You can file a lawsuit against the company, typically if it is less than $5000, you would take it to small claims court where the filing fee is usually less than $100 (even as low as $30 in some counties). Some companies will refund your money right away when they receive the court summons because it would cost them more money to send a representative to defend themselves than it would to refund your money on the spot. Always demand that they reimburse you the filing fee on top of the refund. Hey you gave them many chances to right their wrong, now they have to pay you more or go to court. Debt collectors do the same thing, why can't you?

- You can contact your local TV News Network to file your complaint. This is especially helpful if you know others who have been ripped off by the same company. There is definitely power in numbers with this method, but even if you do not know anyone else who was ripped off by this company, you can still file the complaint. Who knows, maybe other people have filed complaints against this company already and your complaint will open the "Channel Y News Investigates" on the evening news broadcast. The company will be scrambling to get you your refund fast under the threat of media attention. Ouch!

These are not the only tactics you can try. If you have any ideas that are not listed here, try them. If they work, you can write a book too!

As I stated in the introduction of this book, I am tired of seeing people get ripped off, and then not receive their refund. I truly believe if they knew how, they would not give up after the first attempt with customer service or the store manager. That is why I wrote this book. It is my goal to sell over a million copies of this book, and no, it is not because I want to be labeled as a Best Seller. I really can care less about titles or labels. I want to sell over a million copies because I want to make a difference in people's lives and show them how to get their stolen money refunded. I want this book to make a difference in the business world and basically prop up those businesses who practice an honest and ethical business, and eliminate those businesses who are unethical and dishonest. In other words, shape up or ship out.

I appreciate you very much for purchasing my e-book and I hope it made a difference for you and gave you new ideas on how to handle future (or present) rip-off situations. I hope you gained far more value out of this book than what you paid for it.

It is my pleasure to write this book and if I come up with enough new ideas or tactics, I may write a second edition to this book. Until then, visit my blog for recent posts at www.ripofftorefund.net.

Thank You!

www.ingramcontent.com/pod-product-compliance
Lightning Source LLC
Chambersburg PA
CBHW021446170526
45164CB00001B/411